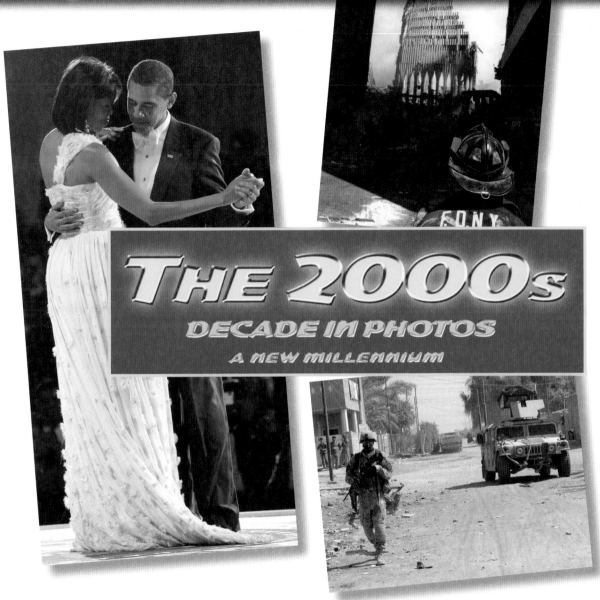

THE 2000s
DECADE IN PHOTOS
A NEW MILLENNIUM

Jim Corrigan

Enslow Publishers, Inc.
40 Industrial Road
Box 398
Berkeley Heights, NJ 07922
USA

http://www.enslow.com

Library of Congress Cataloging-in-Publication Data

Corrigan, Jim.
    The 2000s decade in photos : a new millennium / by Jim Corrigan.
        p. cm. — (Amazing decades in photos)
    Includes bibliographical references and index.
    Summary: "Middle school readers will find out about the important world, national, and cultural
developments of the first decade of the new millennium"—Provided by publisher.
    ISBN-13: 978-0-7660-3139-5 (alk. paper)
    ISBN-10: 0-7660-3139-X (alk. paper)
    1. United States—History—21st century—Pictorial works—Juvenile literature. 2. United States—
Social conditions—21st century—Pictorial works—Juvenile literature. 3. History, Modern—21st
century—Pictorial works—Juvenile literature. I. Title.
    E902.C67 2009
    973.93—dc22
                                                                                          2008054644

Printed in the United States of America.

092009 Lake Book Manufacturing, Inc., Melrose Park, IL

10 9 8 7 6 5 4 3 2 1

To Our Readers: We have done our best to make sure all Internet Addresses in this book were active and appropriate when we went to press. However, the author and the publisher have no control over and assume no liability for the material available on those Internet sites or on other Web sites they may link to. Any comments or suggestions can be sent by email to comments@enslow.com or to the address on the back cover.

Every effort has been made to locate all copyright holders of material used in this book. If any errors or omissions have occurred, corrections will be made in future editions of this book.

♻ Enslow Publishers, Inc., is committed to printing our books on recycled paper. The paper in every book contains 10% to 30% post-consumer waste (PCW). The cover board on the outside of each book contains 100% PCW. Our goal is to do our part to help young people and the environment too!

Produced by OTTN Publishing, Stockton, N.J.

TABLE OF CONTENTS

A hijacked airplane crashes into the south tower of the World Trade Center on the morning of September 11, 2001. Terrorism was a major concern for Americans throughout the 2000s decade.

WELCOME TO THE 2000s

*T*he 2000s were a time of upheaval. Much of that upheaval can be traced to the events of a single day: September 11, 2001. On that day, terrorists attacked the United States. Nineteen men hijacked four airliners, using the planes as bombs to strike targets on the ground. The attacks, which killed almost three thousand people, stunned the nation.

The September 11 attacks had far-reaching effects. President George W. Bush declared a "war on terrorism." In October 2001, he ordered an invasion of

The United States reacted to the September 11 attack by sending troops to hunt down terrorists hiding in Afghanistan. In 2003, American soldiers were sent to Iraq to topple the regime of Saddam Hussein. As the decade ended, U.S. forces were still stationed in both countries.

Afghanistan, whose government was sheltering the terrorist group responsible for the September 11 attacks. Later, in 2003, President Bush ordered the invasion of Iraq. He said Iraq was a threat to the United States, but some people disagreed with the decision to go to war. At home, the U.S. government took steps to prevent more terrorist attacks. Airline passengers faced strict new rules and searches. Congress passed a law, called the Patriot Act, that gave the government more power to collect information on American citizens. It was hoped that this would help catch terrorists before they struck. In a major reorganization of the government, the Department of Homeland Security was created. It is responsible for coordinating efforts to protect the country from terrorism.

If terrorism was a major concern during the first decade of the twenty-first century, it was not the only concern. For years, scientists had been warning that human activities were harming the planet. By burning fuels like oil and coal, scientists said, people were causing temperatures on Earth to rise. This process is called global warming. For a long time, many people denied that global warming was occurring. But more and more people became convinced in the first decade of the twenty-first century. They began looking for ways to use less energy. They recycled. Efforts to help nature were called "going green."

In 2004 and 2005, nature was in the news for a different reason. First, a tsunami struck Southeast Asia. The giant waves swept across the

American athlete Lance Armstrong holds up seven fingers, representing his seven consecutive victories in the most prestigious cycling race, the Tour de France. Armstrong, a cancer survivor, won the race each year from 1999 through 2005.

The 2000s Decade in Photos: A New Millennium

This satellite image shows heat waves being reflected from the Earth. (The blue places show areas covered by thick clouds.) In recent years, people have become more concerned about global warming, an increase in the Earth's average temperature.

Indian Ocean, killing more than 225,000 people. Next, an enormous hurricane battered the southeastern United States. Hurricane Katrina claimed more than 1,500 lives. These disasters were harsh reminders of nature's power.

As the decade closed, energy became a key concern. There was simply not enough energy to meet the world's growing needs. In the past, people relied on oil for fuel. However, the world's oil supply was shrinking. Further, the use of oil added to the problem of global warming. Governments and private companies began looking to tap other sources of energy.

THE USS COLE BOMBING

During the 1990s, a group of Islamic radicals known as al-Qaeda declared war against the United States and its allies. In 1998, this terrorist organization bombed two American embassies in East Africa. Two years later, al-Qaeda terrorists attacked a U.S. warship docked off the coast of Yemen.

Yemen is a country in the Middle East. The USS *Cole* was there to take on fuel and supplies. On October 12, 2000, two men in a small boat approached the powerful warship. They smiled and waved to the sailors, who tried to

Water flows into the forty-foot-wide hole in the side of the USS *Cole* caused by a terrorist attack. Seventeen sailors were killed and thirty-nine were injured in the bombing.

The *Cole* returned to the United States aboard a dry-dock vessel, the *Blue Marlin*. After repairs were completed, the ship returned to active duty in 2002.

warn them to stay away. As the boat drew close to the *Cole*, one of the men pressed a button. It set off a huge explosion. The two men were suicide bombers. When the smoke cleared, there was a gaping hole in the side of the *Cole*. Seventeen U.S. sailors were dead. Dozens more were injured.

The damaged ship began to sink. The surviving sailors worked hard to save it. They succeeded. The USS *Cole* was brought back to the United States. After undergoing repairs, it returned to service.

President Bill Clinton speaks at a memorial service for families and friends of the American sailors killed during the attack on the USS *Cole*.

STYLE OF THE NEW MILLENNIUM

Fashion and music evolved rapidly during the 2000s. Hip-hop clothing remained popular in the early part of the decade. Hooded sweatshirts, or hoodies, were in style. Young people wore them with baggy jeans and designer footwear.

In later years, jeans became slimmer. Young women wore them with flip-flops and crop tops. Men returned to the grunge look of the 1990s. They wore flannel shirts and work boots. Tattoos and body piercings were very popular with both genders. So were vintage styles. Many new clothes were designed to look old and worn.

Young female artists were a driving force in music. The early 2000s saw the rise of Britney Spears, Jennifer Lopez, and Christina Aguilera.

During the 2000s, many young people wore the clothing favored by hip-hop stars: hooded sweatshirts, dark jeans, and sneakers.

Avril Lavigne and Beyoncé soon followed. As the decade ended, young women such as Pink and Rihanna were topping the charts.

The TV show *American Idol* influenced pop music in the 2000s. Winners of the singing contest often went on to stardom. Kelly Clarkson, Jordin Sparks, Carrie Underwood, and Chris Daughtry were a few of the singers who got their start on *American Idol*.

Jordin Sparks is one of many performers who achieved stardom after winning the *American Idol* competition. In 2008 she received an NAACP Award for Outstanding New Artist.

THE DISPUTED ELECTION OF 2000

In November 2000, it was time for Americans to elect a new president. Al Gore and George W. Bush were the candidates for the major parties. The election turned out to be one of the closest—and strangest—in U.S. history.

The Republican Party's candidate, George W. Bush, was the governor of Texas. He was also the son of former president George H. W. Bush. Al Gore, the Democratic Party's candidate, was from Tennessee. He had been the nation's vice president since 1993. Before that, Gore had served in the U.S. Senate.

Over 100 million voters went to the polls on November 7, 2000. Nationwide, Gore had an extremely narrow edge in the popular vote—about 0.5 percent. But the election all came down to Florida, where the voting was so close that officials could not declare a winner. The candidate who won the state would be the next president.

A member of the Palm Beach County, Florida, elections board examines a ballot while other election workers count the controversial "butterfly ballots" used in Florida during the 2000 presidential election. Al Gore's supporters claimed that the confusing design of these ballots caused some people to vote for the wrong candidate.

Demonstrators in Florida protest against the U.S. Supreme Court ruling that stopped the recounting of disputed ballots, December 2000.

Because the election was so close, Florida law said that the ballots needed to be recounted. This was supposed to ensure that all votes were properly counted. By November 10, a machine recount was completed. Bush led by about 325 votes, out of nearly 6 million votes cast. Gore's legal team argued that some of those ballots were counted incorrectly. Several counties ordered ballots to be recounted by hand. Bush's legal team responded by asking a federal court to block the hand recounts. On November 15, Florida's secretary of state, Katherine Harris—who was Bush's campaign co-chair for Florida—announced that she would not accept further recounts from the counties. A week later, however, the Florida Supreme Court ordered the recounts to continue.

Bush appealed to the U.S. Supreme Court. In a five-to-four decision delivered on December 12, the Supreme Court ordered an end to the vote recounts. Florida officials declared George W. Bush the winner. More than five weeks after the election, the country finally knew who the next president would be. On January 20, 2001, Bush was sworn in as president of the United States.

With family members at his side, George W. Bush takes the oath of office as the nation's forty-third president, January 20, 2001.

TV Goes Digital

New technologies enabled manufacturers to develop large flat-screen televisions that offered sharper images than older TV sets.

Television has been a part of daily life since the 1950s. In the 2000s, new technology made TV more popular than ever.

TV adopted the digital technology of computers. The change made room for more channels and better picture quality. High-definition television brought crystal-clear images. Digital video recorders (or DVRs) enabled people to record their favorite shows with the touch of a button. Gaming systems such as Xbox, PlayStation 2, and Wii turned the family television into a hi-tech arcade.

Two girls play tennis on the Wii, a popular video game system produced by Nintendo. By the end of 2008, the Wii was the world's best-selling game system with about 45 million units sold.

By 2003, DVDs had replaced VHS cassettes as the preferred media for home videos.

DVDs made it easy to watch new movies at home. Films about superheroes fueled people's imaginations. So did the Harry Potter movies and the Pirates of the Caribbean films. As the decade ended, it became possible to download movies and TV shows directly from the Internet. New versions of the Xbox and PlayStation allowed players to compete online. Television and home computers were becoming intertwined.

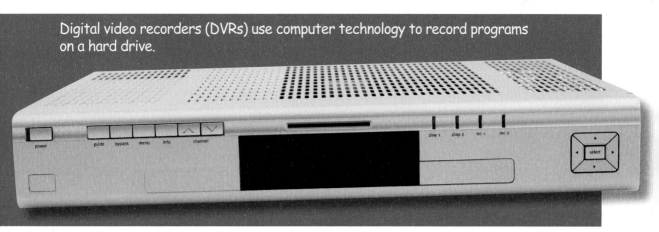

Digital video recorders (DVRs) use computer technology to record programs on a hard drive.

A New York City firefighter looks up at the remains of the World Trade Center after terrorists destroyed the towers.

THE TERROR OF SEPTEMBER 11

By the time of the attack on the USS *Cole* in 2000, members of the terrorist group al-Qaeda were already working on a plan to strike inside the United States. The plan called for hijacked airliners to be flown into buildings.

The term *al-Qaeda* means "the Base" in Arabic. A man named Osama bin Laden created the group. Bin Laden and his followers are Muslims, or believers in the religion known as Islam. But they have radical views that are not shared by most other Muslims.

They believe that Western attitudes and ideas—such as equality for women—are threats to Islam. Using violent means, they want to rid Muslim societies of Western influences. They believe that modern Arab governments are corrupt and not religious enough. They want to overthrow these governments and establish a large Islamic state like the one that ruled the

Pedestrians run from the scene as one of the World Trade Center towers collapses, September 11, 2001.

17

Middle East and North Africa a thousand years ago. To achieve this goal, they believe they must first strike the United States—to force America to stop interfering in the Middle East and to stop supporting corrupt Arab governments.

On the morning of September 11, 2001, two small teams of al-Qaeda terrorists went to the airport in Boston, Massachusetts. They seemed like typical passengers. Shortly after each jet took off, however, the men got out of their seats. Using utility knives as weapons, they seized control of the two airplanes. They steered the jets toward New York City.

Firefighters work at the site where a hijacked airplane crashed into the Pentagon. One hundred and twenty-five people were killed in the attack on the Pentagon.

Once over New York, the hijackers looked for the twin towers of the World Trade Center. The first plane struck the north tower at 8:45 A.M. Less than twenty minutes later, the second plane struck the south tower. Fires in both buildings burned out of control. Before long, the buildings collapsed, killing everyone still inside.

The September 11 terror attacks were not yet over. Two more airplanes had been hijacked. The first jet roared over Washington, D.C. Its hijackers flew the plane into the Pentagon. The final plane never reached its target. The passengers on board fought back. They tried to stop the hijackers. Those terrorists were unable to complete their mission. Instead, they crashed the jet into an empty field in Pennsylvania.

The September 11 attacks killed about 3,000 people. It was the deadliest foreign strike on American soil in history. Many of the victims were firefighters and other emergency workers. They had rushed into the twin towers to save people. The buildings collapsed on top of them. Across the nation, people expressed their sorrow and support. They sent donations for the victims' families. They flew American flags outside their homes. The tragedy united the nation.

Rescue workers look for survivors in the rubble of the World Trade Center a few days after the attack.

STRIKING BACK AT AL-QAEDA

After September 11, President Bush vowed that the United States would fight back against al-Qaeda. He declared a global "war on terrorism." The first step was to destroy al-Qaeda's training camps. They were in Afghanistan, a mountainous country in central Asia.

At the time, a religious group called the Taliban ruled Afghanistan. The Taliban followed a strict Islamic code. They did not let people watch movies or TV. Women were not allowed to attend school. Men had to wear beards of a precise length. Anyone who failed to follow the rules faced harsh punishment. Osama bin Laden supported the Taliban. He used Afghanistan as al-Qaeda's home base.

American leaders suspected that al-Qaeda had been behind the September 11 attacks. The United States offered a large reward for information leading to the capture of the organization's leaders, Osama bin Laden and Aiman al-Zawahiri.

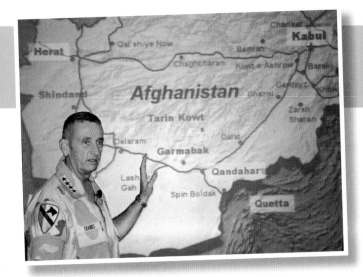

General Tommy Franks discusses the American military operation in Afghanistan, November 27, 2001.

Following September 11, the U.S. government demanded that Afghanistan turn over al-Qaeda's leaders. The Taliban refused. On October 7, 2001, troops from the United States and other nations invaded Afghanistan. They destroyed the al-Qaeda training camps. They also removed the Taliban from power. Osama bin Laden and his aides fled to mountain caves in eastern Afghanistan. Bin Laden appeared to be surrounded, but he escaped into Pakistan.

By 2004, Afghanistan had a new constitution and held presidential elections. But many problems remained. Taliban and al-Qaeda fighters regrouped. They attacked Afghan government forces. They battled American soldiers and the other international troops trying to protect Afghanistan. As the decade ended, the fight to control Afghanistan was still going on.

American soldiers explore the entrance to caves where al-Qaeda and Taliban forces were suspected of hiding, 2002. It did not take long for the U.S. military to drive the Taliban from power in Afghanistan. However, the country's mountainous terrain made it difficult to wipe out the enemy forces completely.

THE DOT-COM BUBBLE BURSTS

The September 11 attacks hurt the U.S. economy. Airlines lost money because fewer people wanted to fly. Other companies stopped hiring new workers. Profits were down. However, the economy was struggling even before September 11. Companies that relied on the Internet were rapidly going out of business.

Most computer, technology, and Internet companies are traded on the Nasdaq stock exchange, shown here. Nasdaq reached its greatest value in March 2000. That month, the dot-com bubble burst. By October 2002, Nasdaq stocks had lost, on average, about 75 percent of their value.

Computer hardware, office tables, and other equipment are ready for auction at the former headquarters of Webvan, a dot-com company that went out of business in October 2001.

The World Wide Web first became popular in the mid-1990s. At that time, many new businesses appeared. Their goal was to make money from the Internet. But in many cases, the companies had no specific plans for how they would do this. Nevertheless, the opportunities for profit seemed endless. Investors eagerly bought stock in Internet companies, creating what came to be called the "dot-com bubble." In economics, a bubble occurs when overly enthusiastic investors drive the price of an asset (such as stock) well above what the asset is actually worth. Some people were willing to pay extremely high prices to own a piece of Internet companies even before those companies had made a single dollar in profits.

By 2001, it was clear that many of the new companies would never make money. The Internet was not as profitable as people had hoped. The companies began going out of business. Their workers were left without jobs. Investors lost their money. The dot-com bubble had burst, helping to drag down the rest of the economy with it. The best Internet companies ultimately survived the dot-com bubble. They include Amazon.com, eBay, Yahoo!, and Google.

Falling stock prices and reports of accounting fraud forced WorldCom, the nation's second-largest telecommuncations company, into bankruptcy in July 2002. The company was valued at more than $100 billion, making it the largest bankruptcy case to that point in American history.

The Dot-Com Bubble Bursts

ERA OF THE GADGETS

During the 2000s, computers kept getting smaller, lighter, and faster. They were no longer bound to the desktop. People began carrying electronic devices wherever they went. It was the era of the handheld gadgets.

Personal digital assistants, or PDAs, were popular at the start of the decade. They had a touch screen for taking notes, making calendar entries, and checking e-mail. As mobile phones improved, they took over many of the PDA tasks. Mobile phones could also take pictures, shoot video clips, and play games.

By the mid-2000s, mobile phones could perform most of the functions of a PDA, such as checking email, browsing the World Wide Web, sending text messages, or keeping track of appointments.

The easy-to-use iPod quickly became the world's most popular digital music player. More than 175 million iPods have been sold since the device was introduced in 2001.

In 2001, Apple Inc. unveiled the iPod. This digital audio player was a huge hit. Suddenly, people could have access to their entire music collection at any time and in any place. Waiting in line at the store became less tedious. So did travel. Portable DVD players enabled passengers to watch movies during long car rides.

For drivers, GPS units made unfamiliar trips easier. GPS stands for global positioning system. A GPS unit uses data beamed from space by satellites. It then displays a map showing which roads to take. As the decade drew to a close, handheld gadgets became a regular part of life.

GPS units help people find their way through unknown areas.

STEROIDS IN SPORTS

A ll athletes want to win. They train hard to be the best in their sport. Some athletes even cheat in order to win. They secretly take drugs that make them stronger and faster. In the 2000s, many sports stars were accused of using anabolic steroids and other illicit drugs. The news shocked and angered their fans.

A drug scandal rocked Major League Baseball in the 2000s. Some players admitted to using steroids. Others denied it, but tests showed traces of

Barry Bonds (batting) won the Most Valuable Player award seven times and ended his baseball career with 762 home runs—more than any other player in history. However, because of allegations that he used steroids, many people feel that Bonds's accomplishments should be removed from the record books.

In 2006, Tour de France officials disqualified the race's winner, Floyd Landis (pictured), because tests showed he had taken performance-enhancing drugs during the race.

steroids in their bodies. Fans expressed disappointment and anger. Many grew skeptical. Whenever a player broke a record, they wondered if he had cheated.

Scandal engulfed other sports as well. In cycling, the winner of the 2006 Tour de France, Floyd Landis, tested positive for drugs. His title was revoked. In 2007, track and field star Marion Jones was stripped of her five Olympic medals because she admitted to having cheated.

Athletes who take illicit drugs risk more than just their careers. They also risk their health. Steroids and other drugs have harmful side effects.

Track and field star Marion Jones wipes tears from her eyes after admitting to using steroids. Because she had cheated to gain an advantage, Jones was stripped of the five medals she had won at the 2000 Olympic Games.

SPACE SHUTTLE COLUMBIA DISASTER

*C*olumbia was America's oldest working space shuttle. It first roared into orbit in 1981. By 2003, it had flown more than twenty-five missions. Then tragedy struck. *Columbia* was returning to Earth after another successful mission. It suddenly broke apart. All seven astronauts aboard were killed.

The accident happened on February 1, 2003. But the problem that caused it occurred sixteen days earlier. During launch, a piece of debris struck *Columbia*'s left wing. The debris made a small hole in the wing. When a space shuttle reenters Earth's atmosphere, it gets very hot. The shuttle's wings are designed to deflect the heat. However, *Columbia's* damaged left wing was not working properly.

Debris from the space shuttle *Columbia* streaks across the sky over Texas, February 1, 2003. The shuttle exploded as it reentered the Earth's atmosphere.

The crew of the doomed shuttle *Columbia* included (front, left to right) mission commander Rick D. Husband, Kalpana Chawla, William C. McCool, (back) David M. Brown, Laurel B. Clark, Michael P. Anderson, and Ilan Ramon.

During reentry, hot gases caused the damaged wing to melt. The rest of the shuttle soon came apart. It burned up in a fireball high above Texas. The *Columbia* tragedy showed that spaceflight is still a risky endeavor. Afterward, NASA grounded its three remaining shuttles. Engineers wanted to fix the problem. Shuttle flights did not resume until 2005. Currently, NASA is designing a new spacecraft to replace the shuttles.

After the *Columbia* explosion, people left flowers, balloons, flags, signs, and other items as a makeshift memorial outside the entrance to the Johnson Space Center in Texas.

A crowd of Iraqis watch as a statue of Saddam Hussein is pulled down in the center of Baghdad, April 2003.

U.S. Troops Invade Iraq

By 2002, President George W. Bush and his aides were publicly making the case for an invasion of Iraq. They accused Iraqi dictator Saddam Hussein of helping terrorists. They said Saddam had ties to al-Qaeda and that Mohamed Atta, the leader of the September 11 hijackers, had met with an Iraqi intelligence officer in April 2001. The Bush administration also said there was no doubt that Iraq had weapons of mass destruction (WMD) and was developing a nuclear bomb.

A squad of American marines advances toward enemy positions near the city of Zubayr in southern Iraq, March 23, 2003. The invasion of Iraq had begun three days earlier. By April 9, coalition forces had occupied Baghdad and forced Saddam Hussein to flee from the capital. On May 1, President Bush declared an end to major combat operations.

Iraq was not permitted to have WMD—which include chemical, biological, and nuclear weapons. In 1990, Iraq had invaded its neighbor Kuwait. The following year, a U.S.-led coalition consisting of more than thirty countries defeated Iraq and freed Kuwait in the Gulf War. Afterward, the United Nations ordered Iraq to destroy all its WMD. UN weapons inspectors were sent to Iraq to make sure Saddam Hussein's government obeyed. But throughout the 1990s, Saddam made it hard for the inspectors to do their job. He told lies and blocked the inspectors from visiting certain sites.

Many people thought Saddam's behavior showed that he was hiding WMD. President Bush warned that the Iraqi dictator might give some of these weapons to terrorists, who could then use them to attack the United States. Bush said Saddam needed to be removed from power before this could happen.

President Bush discusses the progress of the Iraq war with Secretary of Defense Donald H. Rumsfeld (left) and Vice President Dick Cheney (right). American troops carefully searched Iraq for weapons of mass destruction. However, the searches did not uncover the nuclear, chemical, or biological weapons that Bush and his top advisors had expected to find.

In December 2003, American forces discovered Saddam Hussein hiding in a small camouflaged hole near Tikrit. In 2006 an Iraqi court convicted Saddam of crimes against humanity. The dictator was executed on December 30, 2006.

Some people worried about what would happen if the United States invaded Iraq. Would American forces face heavy fighting? And what would happen after Saddam and his government had been overthrown? Would large numbers of American soldiers have to stay in Iraq for a long time to maintain order while a new government was set up? President Bush and his aides did not expect major difficulties. They predicted that the Iraqi people would welcome U.S. forces. Iraqis would be overjoyed to see the removal of their brutal dictator. They would welcome a more democratic government. American troops would be able to leave Iraq a short time after the invasion.

By early 2003, polls showed that about three-quarters of Americans supported an invasion of Iraq. Yet President Bush found little support from other nations. Most felt that there were better ways to handle Saddam. They viewed invasion as a last resort. A few other countries agreed to work with the United States. Allies like Britain, Australia, Spain, and Poland agreed to send troops. The coalition of allies was much smaller than it had been in 1991, however.

Operation Iraqi Freedom began in March 2003. U.S. forces poured into Iraq. They fought hard and defeated the Iraqi army in less than six weeks. But the American mission in Iraq was only beginning.

U.S. Troops Invade Iraq

Chaos in Iraq

On April 9, 2003, American troops rolled into Baghdad. Saddam Hussein had fled the capital city. He was in hiding. Less than a month after the start of the U.S. invasion, the Iraqi dictator had been removed from power.

The Bush administration's predictions of a quick victory in Iraq appeared correct. But signs of trouble soon emerged. There was much looting in Baghdad and other Iraqi cities. Riots broke out. U.S. troops seemed unprepared to stop the disorder.

By the middle of April, the Iraqi army had stopped fighting the American forces. On May 1, President Bush announced the end of "major combat operations" in Iraq.

An Iraqi man prepares to vote in Iraq's first free elections after the fall of Saddam Hussein, December 2005.

An American unit searches for insurgents near Ludifiyah, Iraq. In 2007, President Bush increased the number of U.S. soldiers in the country. This surge of new troops, along with new tactics, helped to reduce the violence in Iraq.

Over the following months, however, American troops faced a different kind of threat. Former soldiers in Iraq's army staged hit-and-run attacks against the Americans. Hundreds of foreign fighters, including al-Qaeda supporters, moved into Iraq. They planted bombs and carried out suicide attacks. Sometimes they targeted American troops. Other times, they killed Iraqi civilians. Iraq is home to several ethnic and religious groups with a history of troubled relations. These groups fought each other fiercely.

The Bush administration hoped that elections would help end the chaos. In December 2005, Iraqis went to the polls and voted for a new government. Yet the violence got worse in 2006.

In January 2007, President Bush announced a troop "surge" in Iraq. By September of that year, about forty thousand more American soldiers had joined the one hundred thirty thousand already in Iraq. At the same time, many Iraqis who had been fighting the Americans joined forces with U.S. troops to fight foreign terrorists in Iraq. Gradually, the violence lessened.

By 2009, Iraq's government had gotten stronger. A new U.S. president announced plans to withdraw most American troops from Iraq by August 2010.

An American soldier speaks with two young Iraqi girls while on patrol in the town of Iman, February 2009.

Hot Issues Divide Society

The 2000s were a turbulent period in the United States. The nation faced many tough issues. Americans disagreed over how to handle these problems. They often argued. Society was sharply divided.

The war in Iraq was a hot topic. Some people felt that the invasion of Iraq had been a mistake. They wanted the U.S. troops there to come home. Other people believed that America needed to finish the job in Iraq. They felt that leaving too soon would help the terrorists who had gone to Iraq after the U.S. invasion. As the war dragged on, these arguments grew more heated.

When the Iraq War began in March 2003, a Gallup Poll found that 75 percent of Americans supported the conflict. By April 2008, however, Gallup found that 63 percent of Americans felt the United States had made a mistake sending troops to Iraq.

People march through Phoenix, Arizona, in support of open borders and unrestricted immigration. Opponents of unrestricted immigration claim that undocumented immigrants take jobs from Americans and increase the cost of education and health care programs.

Americans also debated the problem of illegal immigration. Illegal immigration happens when foreigners enter the country without permission. By the mid-2000s, there were roughly 12 million foreigners living in the United States illegally. Many Americans said these people took jobs that should go to U.S. citizens. Others countered that the immigrants often did work U.S. citizens were unwilling to do. Americans differed about how to stop illegal immigration. They were also unsure of what to do about the illegal immigrants already living in the United States.

People also argued over same-sex marriage. Some said that marriage is meant only for a man and a woman. Others said that two men or two women should be allowed to get married if they wished. Still others did not favor same-sex marriage but did support "civil union." This arrangement would grant same-sex couples rights that married people have. These include the right to make health-care decisions for a partner who is no longer able to make such decisions for himself or herself, or the right to inherit a partner's property without being taxed.

Protestors gather outside the state capitol building in Sacramento, California, to voice their opposition to Proposition 8. This controversial referendum, approved by voters in November 2008, made same-sex marriage illegal in California.

This aerial photo shows the ruins of a village on the western coast of Sri Lanka. In December 2004, Sri Lanka and other Indian Ocean communities were devastated by a deadly tsunami.

DEADLY TSUNAMI OF 2004

*T*sunami is a Japanese word. It means "harbor wave." Tsunamis are rare, but they can be devastating. In 2004, the worst tsunami in history struck Southeast Asia. It killed more than 225,000 people.

Tsunamis start deep in the ocean. An undersea earthquake or landslide triggers them. The sudden movement creates waves on the ocean's surface, much like when a stone is dropped into a pond. Tsunamis start out small.

Residents of an Indonesian community walk through the flooded streets of their town two weeks after it was pounded by the December 2004 tsunami.

At sea, they may only be a few feet high. Upon reaching shallow water, though, the waves grow taller. By the time they reach shore, tsunami waves may be more than fifty feet high.

On December 26, 2004, people were enjoying the warm waters of the Indian Ocean. Beaches were filled with vacationers. As they relaxed in the sun, they had no idea of the approaching danger. A huge earthquake had just occurred far out at sea. It created a series of tsunami waves. The giant waves were rushing toward land.

The beachgoers were puzzled as the ocean suddenly receded. In some places, the water drew back for a mile or more. This was a warning sign, but most people did not recognize it. Then the first wall of water arrived. It was traveling at roughly thirty miles per hour. The powerful wave rushed onto the beach and moved inland. It swept away cars, buildings, and people. More tsunami waves would follow. They surged inland for miles.

Many tsunami survivors had to live in makeshift refugee camps, such as this one in Banda Aceh, Indonesia. The tsunami hit Banda Aceh hard: about one hundred and thirty thousand people living in or near the city were killed.

The 2000s Decade in Photos: A New Millennium

Many countries, including the United States, provided aid to the Indian Ocean communities hit hard by the tsunami. Rebuilding began in 2005 and continues today.

Indonesia suffered the worst damage. Roughly two-thirds of the deaths happened in that nation. Thirteen other countries were also affected. In Sri Lanka, the waves toppled a train, killing most of its passengers. The tsunami fanned out across the Indian Ocean. It killed people thousands of miles away on the coast of Africa. Even nations not struck by the waves suffered losses. Thousands of tourists from Europe were vacationing at Southeast Asian beach resorts. They were among the dead.

The tsunami left more than a million people without homes. These people needed food, drinking water, and medical care. Volunteers from all over the world arrived to help them. Many nations donated money and goods to aid the recovery. The Indian Ocean tsunami was one of the deadliest natural disasters ever. Since then, scientists have worked to identify tsunamis more quickly. They hope to save lives by warning people before the deadly waves arrive.

This aerial view of New Orleans shows the devastating flooding caused by Hurricane Katrina.

HURRICANE KATRINA STRIKES

A hurricane is an immense tropical storm. In August 2005, Hurricane Katrina struck the southeastern United States. It was one of the strongest hurricanes in American history. The harmful effects of Katrina would linger for years.

This satellite image of Hurricane Katrina was taken on August 28, 2005—the day the storm was declared a category five hurricane, with winds up to 175 miles per hour. The next day, Katrina crashed into the Gulf Coast of the United States, causing incredible damage.

Rescue personnel search for survivors of Hurricane Katrina in a flooded New Orleans neighborhood.

The storm first passed over the tip of Florida. It then moved into the Gulf of Mexico. There it grew stronger before making landfall again. Katrina spread damage across several Gulf Coast states. The city of New Orleans in Louisiana was virtually destroyed. New Orleans sits along the Mississippi River near a huge lake. A series of levees, or dikes, protect the city. The massive storm caused these levees to fail. Water surged into New Orleans. Roughly 80 percent of the city was flooded. Hurricane Katrina killed more than 1,500 people. Most of the victims were in New Orleans.

Aerial view of a flooded amusement park near New Orleans in the aftermath of Hurricane Katrina.

After the storm, many Americans were angry with the government. They said that the authorities had not done enough to prevent the loss of life. They were also upset about the government's slow response to the disaster.

Eventually, the residents of New Orleans started to rebuild. Some who were forced to leave during the crisis never returned. The city's slow recovery from the effects of Hurricane Katrina continues today.

A construction crew repairs a flood-damaged house in Biloxi, Mississippi. Many areas of New Orleans and the Gulf Coast are still recovering from the devastating storm.

Massacre at Virginia Tech

Virginia Tech is a college in Blacksburg, Virginia. In April 2007, it became the site of the worst shooting spree in U.S. history. A student armed with two handguns killed thirty-two people. He then took his own life.

Virginia Tech students watch from the entrance to McBryde Hall as police infiltrate the campus, April 16, 2007.

School shootings are a modern problem. They became more frequent in the 1990s. Two Colorado high school students killed thirteen classmates and teachers in 1999. In 2005, a sixteen-year-old boy in Minnesota shot nine people before killing himself. Many other incidents have taken place around the country. School shootings spur debate about gun control. They also raise questions about the impact on young people of violent films and video games.

Seung-Hui Cho, the student who carried out the Virginia Tech Massacre, was twenty-three years old. He had a history of mental illness. On the morning of April 16, 2007, he went to a dormitory and killed two people. He then went to a classroom building and chained the doors shut. He walked through the building, shooting teachers and students. When police arrived, he shot himself. In addition to the thirty-two victims who died, twenty more were wounded. After the shooting, new laws were passed. They make it harder for people who have been diagnosed with mental illnesses to purchase guns.

A student writes on a campus memorial for the thirty-two victims a day after the shooting.

The global energy crisis and concerns about global warming have led many countries to experiment with alternate sources of energy. Enormous turbines like these harness the power of wind to generate electricity.

ENERGY CRISIS GRIPS THE WORLD

Petroleum, or oil, has many uses. It helps grow food, make medicine, and create electricity. It is used to make plastic. Most of all, oil provides power to vehicles. Gas, diesel, and jet fuel are all petroleum products. In recent decades, the world's appetite for oil has grown rapidly. By the 2000s, the world was using more oil than ever before.

Oil is called a *fossil fuel* because it formed underground over millions of years from the remains of ancient plants and animals. For the past 150 years, people have drawn oil to the surface. Each year, the amount left underground has decreased.

By the 2000s, some experts were predicting that the world would begin to run out of oil within a few decades. When the supply of something people need decreases, the price will increase. An increase in oil prices makes many other things more expensive. Rising fuel

When the demand for oil is greater than the supply available, the price of this resource increases.

costs drive up the price of transportation. They also make it more expensive for factories to operate. Businesses must raise their prices to make up for higher costs. As a result, food and manufactured goods become more expensive. As the world's oil supply dwindles, prices can be expected to keep getting higher.

Fossil fuels like oil and coal are also harmful to the environment. When burned, they release carbon dioxide into the air. Carbon dioxide traps heat from the sun, making the Earth warmer. Scientists call this "global warming." Rising temperatures have already begun to melt the planet's polar ice caps. If this process continues, sea levels will rise, flooding coastal areas and islands.

In his award-winning film *An Inconvenient Truth* (2006), former vice president Al Gore explained how fuels like coal and oil produce "greenhouse gases" like carbon dioxide. These gases collect in the atmosphere, where they absorb heat rays from the sun. By retaining the sun's warmth, greenhouse gases cause the Earth's average temperature to rise.

Solar panels like these convert the sun's light and heat rays into electrical energy. Wind power and solar energy are considered "clean" energy sources, because they do not produce pollution or greenhouse gases.

Most scientists also believe that global warming could cause many other serious problems. These include severe droughts in some areas, more-powerful storms in other areas, and the possible extinction of various plant and animal species.

The threat of global warming, combined with a big spike in oil prices in 2008, caused many people to call for changes in the way society uses energy. These changes included the development of cars that are more fuel efficient, as well as greater use of alternative sources of energy. Solar energy uses the sun's rays to make electricity. Windmills create energy from natural breezes. Geothermal power draws natural heat from deep underground. Unlike oil, these sources of energy do not harm the environment. In addition, they will never run out.

ELECTION OF 2008

The United States faced many challenges in 2008. The wars in Iraq and Afghanistan continued. The nation's economy slipped into crisis. Businesses closed, and many workers lost their jobs. During this frantic time, Americans also needed to choose a new president.

The 2008 election was momentous. For the first time, an African American emerged as a leading candidate. Barack Obama was a U.S. senator from Illinois. Before entering politics, Obama worked as a lawyer. Senator John

At the start of the presidential campaign, many people expected that Hillary Clinton (left) would be the Democratic Party's candidate for president. However, Barack Obama's success at organizing volunteers and raising money enabled him to defeat his better-known rival in the party's primary election.

Sarah Palin speaks at a rally in St. Louis as John McCain stands in the background. Palin, the governor of Alaska, attracted a great deal of attention because she was the second woman chosen as the vice presidential candidate of a major political party.

McCain of Arizona was his opponent. McCain, a former Navy pilot, had been a prisoner of war in Vietnam.

For his running mate, John McCain chose Governor Sarah Palin of Alaska. If McCain were elected president, she would serve as the vice president. So even before Election Day, Americans knew they would be making history. They would elect either the nation's first black president, or its first female vice president.

More than 120 million voters went to the polls. The world watched and waited to see who would win. In the end, more people cast their vote for Barack Obama. His message of hope and unity appealed to voters. Obama promised to bring change to the country.

Barack Obama takes the oath of office as the nation's forty-fourth president, January 20, 2009. Obama won easily, receiving 365 electoral votes and 53 percent of the popular vote. McCain received 173 electoral votes and 46 percent of the popular vote.

Looking Back, Moving Forward

*T*he 2000s marked the start of a new millennium. A millennium is a period of one thousand years. The change from old to new millennium caused people to look back on the past. It also prompted them to think about the future.

Humans had made great progress during the previous millennium. There were amazing advances in science, medicine, and art. Leonardo da Vinci imagined brilliant inventions. William Shakespeare wrote beautiful poems and plays. Albert Einstein solved mysteries of the universe. Humanity thrived during this period. In the year 1000, the world's population was about 310 million. By the end of the millennium, that number had grown to more than 6 billion.

The twentieth century saw the greatest progress. From 1901 to 2000, the world changed rapidly. New technology spurred this fast pace. The automobile aided travel. Assembly lines made factories more efficient. Radio, television, and finally computers made it easier to communicate. The rate at which new technologies developed was stunning. At the start of the twentieth century, airplanes did not exist. Less than seventy years later, humans were walking on the moon.

Technology enabled people to reach new heights. However, it did not come without a price. For example, modern weapons made warfare more ghastly than ever. In the twentieth century, two world wars claimed roughly

On January 20, 2009, millions of people visited Washington, D.C., to see the historic inauguration of the nation's first African-American president. In his inaugural address, President Obama called for "a new era of responsibility" and promised to "begin again the work of remaking America."

Laptop computers and mobile phones became smaller and more powerful during the 2000s.

70 million lives. Technology also introduced atomic weapons. These powerful bombs could kill hundreds of thousands of people in an instant. As life was getting better, it was also growing more complex and dangerous.

As the 2000s began, the pace of technological progress remained incredible. Computers kept getting smaller, faster, and more powerful. They helped scientists make new discoveries. Engineers used them to design helpful

A scientist removes embryonic stem cells from a cooler at a research laboratory. Because embryonic stem cells can grow into any type of human tissue, some scientists believe they could one day be used to cure many diseases. However, others object to the use of these cells because the embryo, a living organism, is destroyed when they are collected.

U.S. president Barack Obama (right) speaks with Ban Ki-moon, secretary-general of the United Nations, in March 2009. Since taking office, Obama has worked to improve America's relations with foreign countries, which had suffered during the decade.

new devices. Doctors found amazing new treatments. Computers became a part of everyday life as well. People carried mobile phones, iPods, and GPS units wherever they went.

Yet just as before, technology fostered new problems. Terrorists used cell phones to plan and carry out deadly attacks. Computer hackers could steal data and spread viruses online. A banking and financial crisis threatened the global economy. Many people lost their jobs as companies downsized or went out of business. Modern life also threatened the planet's natural resources. Fuel, clean air, and fresh water were growing scarce. People worried about the Earth's health. Life in the new millennium promised wonderful progress. It also promised thorny new challenges.

CHRONOLOGY

2000—Al-Qaeda bombs the USS *Cole* in October. In November, a major controversy develops around the U.S. presidential election.

2001—George W. Bush is sworn in as president in January. Eight months later, the September 11 terrorist attacks shock the nation. U.S. forces lead an invasion of Afghanistan in October.

2002—In a major reorganization of the U.S. government, the Department of Homeland Security is created to protect America from further terrorist attacks. President Bush also accuses Iraq of producing weapons of mass destruction.

2003—The space shuttle *Columbia* disaster occurs in February. U.S. troops and their allies sweep into Iraq in March. They defeat the Iraqi army in six weeks. Various groups in Iraq begin attacking U.S. forces and each other.

2004—In May, Massachusetts becomes the first state to permit same-sex marriages. George W. Bush is reelected president in November. The Indian Ocean tsunami strikes in December, killing more than 225,000 people.

2005—Space shuttle flights resume in July. Hurricane Katrina batters the Gulf Coast of the United States in August.

2006—The population of the United States reaches 300 million. Former Iraqi dictator Saddam Hussein is executed in December.

2007—The Virginia Tech massacre occurs in April. In December, the Mitchell Report names 89 Major League Baseball players who are suspected of using steroids.

2008—World oil prices reach record highs. The high prices add to a growing financial crisis. In November, Americans elect Barack Obama president of the United States. He becomes the nation's first African-American president.

2009—On January 20, Barack Obama is inaugurated.

GLOSSARY

al-Qaeda—The terrorist group responsible for the September 11 attacks.

anabolic steroid—A synthetic hormone that has an effect on a person's metabolism. Some athletes have abused steroids to increase their strength and muscle mass. However, steroid use can lead to serious health problems.

ballot—The paper or card used to cast a vote.

bankruptcy—A legal condition in which a business or person is unable to pay its debts.

dormitory—A building that houses many students or other persons, often for a temporary period or for a specific event.

embryonic stem cells—Cells produced by an embryo—an unborn human at its first stage of growth—that can develop into any of the more than 220 different cells found within the human body. This ability makes embryonic stem cells potentially useful for treating certain diseases.

geothermal—Relating to the natural heat inside the earth.

hijacker—A person who seizes control of a plane or other vehicle by force.

hurricane—A severe tropical storm that produces strong winds and heavy rain.

levee—A dike or other barrier meant to keep water from overflowing.

millennium—A period of one thousand years.

profit—The money a business earns from the sale of goods or services.

radical—A person with extreme political or religious beliefs.

recede—To move back or retreat.

technology—Society's use of tools and science.

terrorism—The use of violence and fear to achieve political goals.

tsunami—A very large ocean wave, usually caused by an undersea earthquake.

FURTHER READING

Arnold, James R. *Saddam Hussein's Iraq*. Brookfield, Conn.: Twenty-First Century Books, 2008

Davenport, John C. *Global Extremism and Terrorism*. New York: Chelsea House Publishers, 2007.

Englar, Mary. *September 11*. Mankato, Minn.: Compass Point Books, 2007.

Koestler-Grack, Rachel A. *Space Shuttle Columbia Disaster*. Edina, Minn.: Abdo Publishing, 2004.

Lusted, Marcia Amidon. *The 2004 Indian Ocean Tsunami*. Edina, Minn.: Abdo Publishing, 2008.

Marquez, Heron. *George W. Bush*. Minneapolis, Minn.: Lerner Publishing Group. 2006.

Quellette, Jeannine. *Hurricane Katrina*. Edina, Minn.: Abdo Publishing, 2007.

Robson, David. *Steroids*. San Diego, Calif.: ReferencePoint Press, 2008.

Stewart, Gail B. *Life Under the Taliban*. Farmington Hills, Mich.: Lucent Books, 2004.

Worth, Richard. *Massacre at Virginia Tech: Disaster & Survival*. Berkeley Heights, N.J.: Enslow Publishers, 2008.

INTERNET RESOURCES

<http://www.nasa.gov/columbia/home/index.html>
This NASA site honors the seven astronauts who died aboard the space shuttle *Columbia*. Read profiles of the fallen crew members and watch a video tribute to them.

<http://www.nola.com/katrina/>
This site offers fascinating details about Hurricane Katrina. See video of the terrifying storm. View slideshows of the damage in New Orleans. Track the city's recovery efforts.

<http://www.eere.energy.gov/kids/>
This fun site for kids describes ways to save energy at home. Play games, take a quiz, and learn about the future of energy.

INDEX

Pink, 11
politics, 12–13, 52–53
population, 54
public opinion, 36–37

Ramon, Ilan, 29
Rihanna, 11
Rumsfeld, Donald H., 32

same-sex marriage, 37
school shootings, 46–47
September 11, 2001, 4, 5–6,
16–19, 22, 31
See also terrorism
space shuttle *Columbia,*
28–29
Sparks, Jordin, 11
Spears, Britney, 10

sports, 6
and steroids, 26–27
Sri Lanka, 38, 41
steroids, 26–27

Taliban, 20–21
technology, 54, 56–57
digital TV, 14
DVDs, 15
and gadgets, 24–25
television, 14
See also entertainment
terrorism
and September 11, 2001, 4,
5–6, 16–19, 22, 31
and the USS *Cole* bombing,
8–9
"war on," 5–6, 20–21, 31

tsunami (2004), 6–7, 38–41
See also natural disasters

Underwood, Carrie, 11
USS *Cole. See Cole* bombing

Virginia Tech massacre,
46–47

"war on terrorism," 5–6,
20–21, 31
See also terrorism
weapons of mass
destruction (WMD), 31–32
World Trade Center, 4,
16–19
See also terrorism

Yemen, 8

PICTURE CREDITS

Illustration credits: AP/Wide World Photos: 13 (top), 28, 46, 47 (top); Getty Images: 4, 6, 8, 22, 23, 47 (bottom), 52, 56 (bottom); AFP/Getty Images: 17, 27 (bottom), 30; JP Mediainc/iStockphoto.com: 56 (top); Slobo Mitic/iStockphoto. com: 25; Vince Penman/iStockphoto.com: 15 (bottom); Chris Price/ iStockphoto.com: 14 (bottom); Rich Vintage/iStockphoto.com: 24 (bottom); Reuters/Landov: 12; Library of Congress: 13 (bottom); National Aeronautics and Space Administration: 7, 29; National Oceanic and Atmospheric Administration: 43; used under license from Shutterstock, Inc.: 10, 11, 14 (top), 15 (top), 24 (top), 26, 27 (top), 36, 37, 38, 40, 48, 49, 50, 51, 52 (top); United Nations photo: 38, 41, 57; U.S. Department of Defense: 1 (top left, bottom), 5, 9, 18, 20, 21, 32, 33, 34, 35, 42, 44, 45, 53 (bottom), 55; U.S. Marine Corps photo: 31; U.S. Navy photo: 1 (top right), 16, 19, 39.

Cover photos: U.S. Department of Defense (Obama inauguration, soldiers on patrol), U.S. Navy photo (September 11).